Susan Wicks grew up in Kent and studied French at the Universities of Hull and Sussex, where she wrote a D.Phil. thesis on the fiction of André Gide. She has taught in France and at University College, Dublin. She now lives with her husband and two daughters in Tunbridge Wells, and works as a part-time tutor for the University of Kent.

by the same author

SINGING UNDERWATER

OPEN DIAGNOSIS

Susan Wicks

faber and faber
LONDON · BOSTON

First published in 1994
by Faber and Faber Limited
3 Queen Square London WC1N 3AU

Photoset by Wilmaset Ltd Wirral
Printed in England by Clays Ltd St Ives plc

Susan Wicks is hereby identified as the author of this work in
accordance with Section 77 of the Copyright, Designs and
Patents Act 1988.

A CIP record for this book is available from the British Library

ISBN 0-571-17139-7

2 4 6 8 10 9 7 5 3 1

for Alison Townsend

Acknowledgements

Poems from this collection have appeared in *Ambit, British Council Anthology of New Writing 3, London Review of Books, Observer, Poetry Durham, Poetry East* (USA), *Poetry Review, Spokes, Sunday Times, The Women's Review of Books* (USA) and *Yankee* (USA).

I should like to thank Cottages at Hedgebrook for providing me with time and an incomparable space in which to write a number of these poems.

Contents

III

I

Bear Country

This is bear country, forest of eyes
and fur, all the black rainbow
from coal-dust to cinnamon.
Trees bristle, rub themselves
electric in shadow. This
is what dark is. Starlight
turns my hair white as I crouch,
pans gold in my small puddle.
In the tent my sleeping daughter
sniffs, grunts, rolls into dream again
under her borrowed ceiling of canvas,
sees the brown skin of marshmallows
blister in the heart of campfires.

Seeing with Hands

She plays at Helen Keller,
measuring the unfamiliar
rooms, eyes shut, touching
their dark furniture.

She walks stumbling on treasure —
a stamp, a coin, a needle —
crouches with spread fingers,
breathing the floor's honey.

Will she learn the stiff reek
of love on sheets, know the night
rhythms, read the bumps
on recurring faces?

Outside she crumples red-gold
and russet, shreds paper
veins between her fingers,
feels the seed-pods rattle.

We watch her through glass,
distrust our adult senses
to spell out 'water' when
the pump groans and spits silver.

Gaining Entry

After eighteen years of marriage
I come home to you
with no key; my repeated hammering
will not rouse you, the double ring
of the telephone sounds
endlessly in your hall. Dark knots
of well-meaning neighbours
with flashlights, advice, ladders, try
your locks and sashes, want
to bring us together. Crunching on cinders
between walls and leaning fences,
I lead the featureless procession
to where a window,
blank over shadow-limbs and flowers,
closed on its swell of breathing,
shudders to the fist of the stranger
on the top rung – sticks, creaks,
opens on our daughter,
her pink midnight face,
her pink pyjamas
in the gap between curtains.

Husband Worship

When I swim, I can see you
from underneath, a huge fish
returning, breaking back into the water,
ploughing your furrow of bubbles.
At the end, you turn from me
without seeing, bury yourself sleepily
in ripples and glide away from me,
your close head with the goggles
reappearing in the intervals
of your stroke like a stranger's.
If I want to make you see me
I must stand at the rail before you,
so you bump into me. You falter,
rise, spit, say, 'Only eleven more.'

Cutting Your Hair

I follow the soft valley of your
nape, parting the hidden
shafts to the scalp, white and unwrinkled
as the skin of a boy I once saw
shivering on a field, his hair
teased into rosettes like a guinea-pig's.

You lean forwards for me, your back bony
as the body of a boy
crouched on wet sand to hold back
the sliding ramparts, a scummy trickle
veining the sleek water.

With the scissors I make you
new, your bent head
close as a baby's. Standing
to explore it with your man's fingers,
you look down at what I have cut off,
thanking me through a fine rain of needles.

Sleep

Our bedroom that year would hardly
let us sleep. Across the white bedspread
the snow-light would run in rivers
as we tossed to the crack and creak
of hardwood. At 2 a.m. we would surface
to the water-softener's slow rush,
waking us into dark, a displaced morning.
Sometimes from the night bedside
a Midwestern voice would ask us,
'Is Bobby there?' Once, on an afternoon
when white sun fell through the leaves
of the maple and kids cried out
at baseball, the curly flex connected
me to death like an umbilical.

On the wall
by the dry splash of last summer's mosquito
the Georgia O'Keeffe iris was
secret and erectile, its sleep-coloured fissure
rising from vague leaves as if to stand
for the shape of all dreaming.

Voice

In the garden shed, among flower-pots,
his words explode into her:
You fucking cow, you came out here
just to . . . all you fucking wanted . . .
As I peg out the laundry
I hear him still haranguing
silence, her answers whispered so low
they could be absence. He pauses
to pant and breathe and she
emerges, head bowed, carrying a teacup.

Later I hear them in their adjacent
bedroom, their old bed-springs
creaking, his spent mouth finally
quiet, as a new voice gurgles and rises
in her throat, calling
like a muezzin or a goatherd,
bridging the strange intervals.

You Hate Me

Each night we walk out
into the darkness, our combined shadow
mincing and scraping before us
on wet pavements. You hate me. You loiter
in shop doorways, duck in to pee behind
thick hedges, call women from public boxes.
I memorise the wine-labels in the window
of the off-licence, yearn between curtains
for the warm flicker. You hate me.
We kick beer-cans into the front gardens
of semi-detached houses. Our fists rattle
the metal teeth of slot-machines, we spray
'Fuck' into the dark glass
flank of a bus-shelter. You wrench
signs to unnatural positions, suck
bollards from concrete. I decapitate
daffodils, strip the green bark
from saplings. Together we sit
on the kerb laughing and crying. You
hate me. I am sick
into the gutter. We
start for home. I turn
the key in our dark lock,
open the door, reaching for all the switches.

In White

Here where all movement
is unstoppable, I kick footholds
in ice, press myself into hardness.
A wild heartbeat
could surely unbalance us. I reach, tense,
touch you, the two of us one tangle
of broken body
as the cloud parts under us
on pylons, a dark fur of young larches.

Later I learn the secret
under your skin, the shapely
ball of your right shoulder
in its socket, the fine crack
of light that will fuse so sweetly.
Through falling snow
I follow the doctor's pointing finger
as he asks, Do I think I can find it,
the one pharmacy still open in the village?

Through a net of falling whiteness
I look past him
between ski-racks and shop-windows
for the gap between buildings.
My teeth chattering, I rifle
your warm pockets for cash, assure him
I will, I will.

Trying to Make Green

PARANOIA

You didn't recognise them at first, the warders,
before they wore uniforms, when the older one
would smile into his cider, before he smoked
twenty a day in the yellow cave of his fingers,
and the younger one only a baby
you passed between you, needing hardly
more than milk and your arm's circle
for his hungry body. The same cell
was airier in those days, there were curtains
lifting in sunlight. You seem to remember
green plants; birds would come sometimes
to flutter the crumbs offered on the sill.
Now strange men patrol at your windows,
sleep in your beds, mark your poor furniture,
coil their grey breath nightly to the ceiling.

Since you left, your kitchen has turned
yellow, the ceiling a textured abstract
of grease and nicotine, the ring-scars
intersecting across your table.

Your plants grow jaundiced, the tea-towels
crease to a rope of twisted ochre.
Your hooded windows are a benighted
squint of smoked gold. Now you

enter your own house like a visitor,
see how your young self leans her elbow
on the table's blank formica
to watch her children mix colours;

how the clear green still escapes them
as they dip and scrub their thick brushes
in sepia messes; how the sky wavers
with brush-marks, hairs trapped in the blue.

DRINAGH

If I could lift you up
and set you down in Drinagh
where the sky is more sky
for floating in cobalt water

set you down in Drinagh
where the old trees hunch
in the shape of the wind
and you would run with your brother

in Drinagh where there may still be children
to go barefoot to school
with potatoes in their pockets
and the light through the fuchsia hedges
is still green, whether or not you remember

where your girl's name still lingers
and doors would still start open
on faces to cry and exclaim over
if I could lift you up
and set you down, and you could remember.

STORY TIME

What story are they listening to, to make the baby
chew her soft clown, the little girl's fine hair
rise as if in fright, hands clasped across soft tartan
in her lap? Does the witch lean from her high tower

to claw at them, these three rapt faces
captured on paper: already they almost follow
the crumbs on the path, the silk plaited to ladders,
stones rolling and rattling in a belly.

The boy sits like a tailor, the small stiff jeans
creasing in miniature, the escaping collar,
the scaled-down cable on the small sweater.
He listens. He resembles his father, already

he is like his grandmother in her ward where no one
listens. Light glances. A glass mountain? In soft focus
the chair-legs, the buggy, the mother's wrist at rest,
the baby's soft shoes that have not yet seen dancing.

'My Gift to the World'
(*Hans Andersen*)

Elder and willow, elder and willow,
from a small stick to a spreading tree,
child to wife to grandmother,
cut me and embed me and I grow again.

Willow and elder, willow and elder,
out over the flowing water,
make my flesh into whistles.
Long leaves fall and come, fall and come.

Man and wife, man and wife,
poverty to cream in the cool dairy.
Cattle in the green meadows,
river low under the old trees.

Child and willow, child and willow,
break me loose from the leaning trunk.
Strip me and float me out on the water.
Let me streak away over the clear stones.

II

Plates
(*to Alison*)

When they gave you your plates
to hand on to some new doctor,
you held them up to the window
and saw the sky in them,
the river running through your skull,
twigs meeting at the cerebellum,
your brain uncurling, tentative
as a snail on its late glide-path.
Since then I have often thought
of snails and their reflexes,
seeing a slice of America
green through your head's filter.

Ticking Hands

Today the world is white and set
in its mask, trees ready to pivot
towards spring, the slow push of green
a blur under domed glass.

This is a timer's face, blank
and accurate as quartz, winter branches still
at ten and two, as the linked shadows
move on a frozen surface.

My limbs tick the hours, my left hand
conscientious and companionable
as Big Ben timing the tide-swing at Waterloo.
The bridge slides under departures,

its narrow band of stiffness cracked
and intimate as old leather. No panic.
No pigeons. My hands only twitch quietly,
measuring the white hiatus.

Motion-sickness

This is a station like any other,
the illegible place-name sliding,
the spaced lamps, the posters
of mountain-climbers' landscapes
somewhere in Wales, the night
sleeper worming its glow-path
through darkness. There is even
a buffet of familiar faces
mirrored in urns; invisible trays
shunt one another gently
towards the till. A few stragglers
still collect up their belongings,
turn from our door-slam and whistle
to catch a late connection.
A woman in a raincoat shakes
out a buggy one-handed, pacifies
her disappearing child with a lolly.

This is a journey like any other:
my body sways over sleepers,
judders at points, shakes to time
and distance. On its rest my left arm
jerks, a seasoned traveller –
will not stop now until our train
glides in under the glass canopy.

Growing Cold

I always relished the cold, watched
forecasts avidly, loved how the winter
worked its transformations, bared
trees, ruffled feathers, filming
the pond with slow cataracts.
We spoke through clouds, walked
doggedly, in no one's footprints.
Here the cold is a quite different
animal: breath-marks inside
storm-windows, howling, flesh
bitten. Still I study forecasts,
the lilac, the little numbers,
the child's sun smiling
through snowflakes. As it grows
colder – twenties, tens, single
digits – and the year settles,
packed hard as frozen meat, I clap
hands, feel my raw fingers twitching.

Communion

We ate our last celebratory
supper with a cripple
drawn up to the table
in a wheelchair, his little legs
tucked under, pigeon feet
strung inwards as if to touch
each other, the long left wrist
bent back, searching.
Tides of saliva sucked
and fell, glinted at the edges
of his laborious words.
When we were all finished,
he still had a plateful
to guide upwards with his good hand.
When we fell silent
his creature voice croaked,
swelling in all our spaces,
the bright thread of his spittle
spinning in the air between us.

Homing

Right in a strange country
was left in some lost cell.
I catch myself on corners
trying to look both ways:
on a stranger's bicycle
I circle endlessly
before I can be sure of leaving
in the appropriate direction.
In my last note home
I wrote 'dady' for 'baby'
and let the rogue letters fly
like a pair of silly pigeons.

When a door against me
says HƧUꟼ, I push.

Vocabulary

These flora and fauna have no names:
crimson-bodied, orange-throated,
black-gold mosaic-winged,
straight-stemmed, shrill-voiced,
they mass in skeins, packs, shoals,
howl through dark or flash silver,
bending, beating, reflected in still water.
Later I learn them from books:
cardinal, Indian paintbrush, coyote –
match each with an image and mount it
in sequence on blank paper: cholinesterase,
multiple sclerosis, poison oak.

To Remember

This is not the *Titanic*
because there are no icebergs
in Lake Michigan in summer
to block out stars from portholes
with a sheer face of darkness,
no deep shudder
from keel to crow's nest, no scrape
of nails on locked doors between decks;
no women or children screaming
audibly; there are life-preservers
forwards at all levels – they told us –
and only a brass quintet
of high-school teachers
on vacation to play us out
to new journeys, absences,
a call between two continents,
as we chew on fried chicken,
pour wine from brown paper.
It was too late then, surely,
to watch a thin sunset
push out from its belly of raincloud.

And besides, we are not 'unsinkable',
and it couldn't have been Bach *they* were playing.

World

This is the world.
Eat it quickly
segment by segment
before it shrivels.

This is the pith
clinging to your fingers
in bitter tatters
every white scrap.

This is the smallest pip,
sclerotic raindrop
full of forgotten
juices. Crack it open.

Imaging

We sat in each other's arms
on the couch to watch *2001*, the white planets
waltzing to Strauss, the weightless
travellers, their breath freezing
on little windows, as we waited
for the one moment when Hal would sing
'Daisy', his mind slipping out in segments,
juicy as a blood-orange.
And we savoured
the rainbow plunge into light,
the eye blinking into focus,
the purple and yellow landscape of destination.

Tight in my time-capsule,
head taped to this strange pillow,
I blink blue and gold,
violet, magenta, as a well-placed mirror
shows me creatures from Jupiter
who move behind glass and measure,
then trundle me into air again,
empty me into a strange century,
my brain imaged on a screen behind me.

I know what they see
of a woman's head, poor world
careening into the dark,
white seeds sleeping under the surface:
they see the future, earth-
landings, slow waltzes, time-travel,
while I still squint and blink
at the gift of so much colour.

Germinal

This is my disaster.
The props were worm-eaten.
The roof fell in predictably.

I smell it coming like water
or fire in dry wheat-stubble,
the rush of air in the lift-shaft.

Pushing into hot earth
with the dust-screen behind me,
I can hear blind horses choking.

The sweat runs, stripes me
black in waves. My face bleeds
the mine's own colours.

At the end of the tunnel
I take out my flask, tear
my wedge of bread into daily pieces.

Here is the place, the perfect
platform, where I huddle,
hallucinating, thirsty for surfaces,

and wait for the warm tide to cover
my feet, my ankles; the intimate
nuzzle of an old lover's body.

Caul

My father was born in a caul. For years
my grandmother kept it in attics,
shrivelled like a giant foreskin,
against some future drowning.
Once, as a young man, gasping,
he must have cried for it, his lungs
pressed flat as flowers between
two weights of salt water. until
he surfaced and his friends caught him.

Now his only daughter
has M.S. He still lights bonfires,
potters to the back door for matches,
coughs as swallows swim up in blue air.
He is old now. I could almost
blow dust from the wrinkles,
stretch the small bag to cracking
as it gaped to hold him,
wrap his porous bones tight in a dry skin.

Propaganda

(to my father)

Before I was born, you flew
over strange countries, mapped
strips of foreign earth and shuttered
cottages, plotting your course
by the stars. No bombs:
you towed gliders, you told me,
brought supplies to families
in need; dropped only
packets of unseen messages
to a tangle of gorse and heather,
bricks of paper
that fluttered apart in your slip-stream.

Now, in your peace-time,
what should I drop on you –
falling leaves, fliers, sweets
for the big-eyed children? Or
a sheaf of spiralling photographs
black with blood:
Nicht Euer Kind,
Nicht Euer Kind,
Nicht Euer to gape at you
as you shuffle home,
from a thorn-hedge or a puddle?

Or nothing,
my head to the chute
as I look down
at the blind villages
under my precious cargo.

Correspondence
(*to J.S.*)

You told us your mother should have
shot herself at a precise moment
some time after the diagnosis,
letting the bullet carve her head
into space for her growing children.

I catch myself smiling, as I tell you
we don't carry guns in England
and you write, 'Don't worry, it's not time
    yet,'
lean back in your chair to chuckle.

In our downstrokes I see her,
on sofas, in a vintage wheelchair,
the locked drawer you could never
turn your back on. Funny how
she walks the Atlantic
in both directions,
making us both laugh.

Glad Game

('. . . *euphoria, which has been said to go with having M.S. . . .*')

Some joker has given me a rainbow-maker,
souvenir of America. Strung up in my window
it burns flags into the spines of paperbacks,
throws up a mess of sunsets.

On good days my brain also makes rainbows,
dashes its handful of crystals on glass;
my head is all flecked with coral, magenta,
indigo, such gorgeous dandruff.

Even as a child I could surely muster
a wince, learning how Pollyanna
split sun miraculously,
cured life with colours
and the tinkle of cut glass,
dismantled whole chandeliers;
even then I must have thought her

very American.

How to Become Invisible

Dress carefully. Choose
the faded childhood anorak,
the torn skirt with the fringes.
Take a container for pennies,
something to drape over you, honeycomb
blanket or gaping mackintosh, a grip
for your possessions.
Squat on bridges in the shelter
of low walls. Don't look at the water.
Be ill or crippled. Find a few children
to skulk at your ankles like pickpockets.
See briefcases, the silver flight of pigeons,
bunches of tight daffodils.
Practise the patter in odd moments.
Bring something you can sing to.
Play musical instruments.

Buying Fish

I am one of you, though you do not
know it. We are all hesitant, we are all
gentle and elderly. Together
we point and stutter. Our string bags wait
for wet parcels, gape to receive
the same slippery gift. Tonight we shall all
search our mouths for bones,
as the fragile skeletons
are picked clean, discarded, wrapped in plastic
to cheat the rough tongues of cats. I am
one of you. Watch me buy a thin fillet
of plaice for my single serving, drop keys, fumble
the change. I can beg as well as you
for a few sprigs of sour parsley. I can look
a whole slab of rainbow
trout straight in the eye.

Strawberry-picking

One day a man came to us
with a small jar, asking permission
to scatter his mother's ashes
in the light that lay like dust
between the rows of Red Gauntlet.

Then we picked strawberries
as if an old woman knelt with us
on that sun-striped hillside,
watching our fat fruit mount
in punnets, eyeing the most luscious,

pouncing on straw, slugs, bird-pecks
our young hands had passed over,
reading weights over our shoulder
till the farmer called out, 'Time,'
and we walked to where the wind couldn't blow her.

A disabled toilet is

wider than for ordinary
women because you would need more
space a sloping polished
rail in case you should suddenly
reach out even the paper dispenser
fuller the shiny black floor
twice the width in case you should suddenly
dance slide pirouette see
a whole line of faces in it
roll about laughing
even the graffiti
scratched at ground level you could
make noises grunt heave
gargle your saliva to a tune from *Carmen*
until ordinary women
got down on their knees to peer under
your locked door at wheels
drawn up to the high pedestal.

Blind Skiers

We shrink at the edge
of the piste to avoid them, the blind
skiers with their fluorescent lettering.
This sheer white space
is theirs to practise survival on,
tilting into emptiness –
our hairpin of imagined traverses.

With a soft crunch
they leave us standing, where we can see
white hills and gulleys, sun,
the deeper white of shadows,
our skin burned visibly.

They lean out into the valley
where a sprawl of villages
sleeps already in starlight.
Under their feet the moguls
flex curves of dark muscle.
Black snowflakes melt against their faces.

Re-entry

Rewinding the taped
music I first heard the evening we came down
from Alpe d'Huez, I see winter
change to spring as we lose height,
ferns grow like human hair
after death, unknown flowers
sprout where the black snow ends.
Our double-decker
sways slightly over the impossible
drop, slows at each hairpin, almost
to a standstill, levels like a lost heartbeat —
picks up its laborious zigzag,
another few metres. Leaf-buds
brush the window, burst, twist open
as it unwinds again slowly, this record
of time spent in a cold place —
how we said goodbye to everything —
how we came back to meet the flat fields,
our feet swinging over young larches,
birdsong rising from the valley.

Coming Out

I have always been
this. I have always
had an invisible limp,
a peripheral numbness, always
seen men tower over me,
as if from a wheelchair. I am
already blind, have always
mistaken the necessary places,
never been good enough
at guiding food to my mouth,
finding the exit.
This is what I am. I already
speak as if drunk, stain
my bed each night
as I dream. Now I can say it
quite openly: as I
came out for those last
tests, wiping raindrops
from my high saddle
under blue sky, I could have
smiled, laughed, sung
all the way to the hospital.

Message from Galena

In the blue pool, her body
was like anyone's, flattened as ours were
by refraction, fish-pale, only the water
making it monstrous. She swam
almost as we swam, one leg trailing
imperceptibly, cutting through
light as we all did. In the changing-room,
walking slowly with a stick, she would still
walk almost as we walked, her wet body
glowing, leaving a line of footprints.

In that other pool in Galena,
Illinois, I couldn't watch him
as he lowered himself from his wheelchair
to the steps, his heavy torso waiting
as the water danced, its white ripple of
chain-mail ready to wrap him. I couldn't
watch him, couldn't look at
even the empty chair, the long vista
to the lake, down through bare branches.

And yet I am still swimming
as I have always swum since childhood,
feeling something like seaweed between my toes,
still breathing, combing the cold with my fingers,
as my weed collects other weed,
and trails out behind me,
waving green, dark rust,
hosting barnacles, whelks, winkles, mussels.

When I am blind I shall

paint pictures: take a step backwards,
point my brush like a knife and dare
the canvas to come closer, all my creations –
fruit, flowers, fields, clouds,
nudes – stippled all over
with wet sunlight pungent as leaves,
as I touch here, and here, and here, as we used to
pin tails on donkeys.

When I am blind I shall not

write in colours. As I come down
over the headland, the bay's silver
surprises me, and the blue mountains,
the white-rimmed clouds, the black
of high fir-trees, the road-signs
like mustard. I shall write sun
and shadow by the sweat on me,
hills by my heartbeats, the angle
at my ankles, write this other landscape
by smell, the taste of
salmonberries, hearing the birds
and the wind always, the shriek
of a July firework echoing on a barn,
the beep-beep-beep of something heavy reversing.

Carpenter Ant

You and I are of one mind. Poisons
set for you have sent my brain
scuttling backwards. Preserving
their precious houses, men would kill
your long dark thorax,
your quick running legs,
your black egg of abdomen. Here we share
time, air, sunlight. Soon you start
the long march back
to the splintered heart of dwellings. Let me
offer you my hand
to crawl, scuttle, run, dance over,
the sun glancing from your quick body.
You and I will measure
this space together: carpenters
have occasionally produced
miraculous furniture.

Walking Too Far into the Island

You will take a child's back-pack and walk
into the island, step off into these long foreign
verges of seed-grasses to let the heavy trucks
pass you on the highway, metalled and barren

as your other life, and bear east, seeds itching
in the folds of your socks, your looped shoe-laces. You will
pull your hat down over your eyes, squatting
in a wood to relieve yourself between trunks, your full

bladder emptied furtively over needles; stumble
as you emerge, readjusting the straps to your shoulders,
to discover lakes — a prey to cruising rednecks,

bunches of biking kids almost wilder
than the place itself. You will not panic
to notice your own dead feet striking between brambles.

On Being Eaten by a Snake

Knowing they are not poisonous,
I kneel on the path to watch it
between poppies, by a crown of nasturtiums,
the grey-stripe body almost half as long
as my own body, the formless black head
rearing, swaying, the wide black lips seeming
to smile at me. And I see
that the head is not a head,
the slit I have seen as mouth
is not a mouth, the frilled black under-lips
not lips, but another creature dying; I see
how the snake's own head is narrow and delicate,
how it slides its mouth up and then back
with love, stretched to this shapelessness
as if with love, the sun stroking
the slug's wet skin as it hangs
in the light, resting, so that even the victim
must surely feel pleasure, the dark ripple
of neck that is not neck lovely
as the slug is sucked backwards
to the belly that is not belly, the head
that is merely head
shrinking to nameable proportions.

III

First Poem

They found their first country, found
gardens, a white landscape, snow-covered, no
mother. Their widowed father
must have created it, their two soft bodies
purple with frost, mottled, the tree
strung with ice, the brittle apple
glass-coated. As he bit into it
it splintered. When she held it
she left her own finger
stuck to the dark surface
to fall and be buried
by blizzard. And he remembered
how God had peeled back
the skin over ribs, how they had shivered
uncontrollably, gone almost mad
with cold as she had met him, their teeth
rattling, tongues like sucked icicles. Leaving
the footprints, the core, her small finger
still clinging, they knew only
a thousand words for snow: the fur
leaves that would cover their crotches
were very welcome.

Breast Envy

At eight I already dreamed
of breasts, full warm moons
in eclipse like my mother's,
her valley of skin, the unthinkable
red blisters of sun-spots
at each nipple, the buried blue rivers
streaking the pale surfaces.

I already had visions
of how we would all possess them,
every one of us, how we would
snake across the playground in a milky
galaxy, while you would all stand
in your dark line for ever, with not
a breast between you.

And I remember
how we once half-
mutilated ourselves in a
long ripple of night grasses
so we might carry arms; how you also
mutilated yourselves to the tears of candles
so you could sing.

Hangman

Some nights in the train we would play
hangman, our heads close together
as out in the corridor
a line of boys in dark flannel
turned their backs. From a suggestion of bodies
stick limbs pushed out, feet, the reprieve
of fingers. Over our bent heads
the half-heard questions circled:
'Was he . . . ?', 'And how long . . . ?',
'How far did you . . . ?'

Some nights on the landing
between bedroom and bathroom
my father would bend to kiss me
goodnight, the answer of his pale body
swinging in the dark between us
like a fish on a hook.

The Laughter of Dentists

Since there is so much laughter
in dentists, it was hardly surprising
to hear how that master-craftsman
of amalgams and crowns and bridges
had removed his long white rubber
gloves for his dental-nurse mistress,
how they sat in his surgery together
each night after the last departure
and breathed gas, undressing each other,
laughing uncontrollably at cavities,
haunted by high-speed screaming,
chipped enamel, abscesses, root-fillings,
the stretched mouth of pain under them,
that could rise at the touch of a button.

Hitler and His Mother

'A l'heure où je vous parle, Hitler s'est endormi
en suçant son pouce . . .'
Patrick Modiano, La Ronde de Nuit

Did even Hitler have a mother
to feed him and wrap him in towels,
lower him to the rusty water,
while above him the geyser
snorted its hot message? Did he lie there
and splash gently, bending his fat knees,
squealing as she sponged suds over him
like another skin, soaped him
in the folds of his chin like a baby?
Did he look up at the ceiling,
follow the old cracks running
from one corner, forking towards sounder
plaster? Did he see spiders? When she
lifted him and folded him to her
did she play counting-games with him —
church, steeple, clergyman,
little piggies — call him
the cleanest one in the family,
show him his white skin all wrinkled
as the water ran off him in rivers,
dance like a child with him,
tell him he had washerwoman's fingers?

Hamilcar's Daughter
(*after Flaubert*)

It is about a girl standing on a staircase
hung with figureheads. It is about gardens,
the slow sunset over terraces.

It is about a slave's speeches,
purple, ivory, gold, spices; about weeping
skin, the oiled Suffete in his close litter.

It is about entry through echoing channels
to the secret, fur-carpeted passages
alive with sparks, the reptile's

cold slither between chained ankles.
It is about the unthinkable
veil of the Goddess, a river

rusty with corpses,
the torn ears of elephants, a parched
city besieged by black skeletons.

It is the death-prayer in the young girl's
curtained alcove. It is the high panic
of a pack of skittering monkeys

with familiar faces. It is history. It is
palaces, pits, pavilions, mercenaries,
eaters of unnamed delicacies.

It was the pattern of shells at the threshold,
her holy fish massacred in the fountain.

First Coming

She might have been sleeping on a flat roof
or making bread, or pounding the wet linen,
her back turned to Him in an arched doorway,
or singing as she walked home carrying water.

There was no time to wonder if she knew Him,
if He was the father of someone close to her,
no time to gasp, or cry out – before He was on her
like a robber, pinning her wrists and burning

His precious liquid into her
like acid or molten metal or the swarming points
of hot starlight. She bit down
on His tongue, and found her mouth full of

nothing, she pushed at Him
with all her frantic fingers, and met
no resistance, as her body let down its mane of bright
blood, rasped by a swollen emptiness.

What she heard
was her own voice, her own breathing
as He etched His need into her, and withdrew,
the dry streams still criss-crossing her like a delta.

Now she can sing
her magnificat – sing it each morning
as she bends over the cool basins,
her hair sticking to her cheeks, her new body

shaking, as if it did not belong to her.

Life

Since I found out you were pregnant
I have wanted to pick you up and take you
to some high studio lit from the sky,
arrange your pale limbs against draperies
and see sun curl across them; when you first
told me your trouble, I wanted
to place you in sunlight, let the sun
round out your belly, the wry curve
of your cheek, see the dust dance
over you in a sun-shaft; I wanted
to carry you long steep flights upwards
to where an improbable easel stood
waiting, stretching its tired canvas,
so I could paint light
touching your body like a knife,
stroking you open with its twin edges –
till the foetus thrashed into life, and you came
to peer over my left shoulder
at love gleaming like a good apple
from a flat surface, its dark pips hidden
in pale flesh and smooth skin, unmistakable.

Inheritance

They are the real fliers,
these infants in back-carriers,
Moses baskets: through sun
and mackerel cloud they never wake,
faces squashed into arm-rests
or the hollow of a mother's
shoulder as we travel
back into daylight. Over Seattle
we bank. Sun reels on our ceiling,
and they hang level
in a hammock of warm skirt,
still rock on the home runway.

When lights flicker our final
descent, will they still be
above us, so many blind cherubs rising
and falling, sucking the thin air
like milk? When we hit
will they follow us
more gently, their sleepy
pucker of mouth leaving
soft prints on mountains?

Twin Otters

If we could curl ourselves simply
together, as these bronze otters do
on a rock over water, our dark bodies
sleek in their patina
of bruises, our blunt
muzzles parallel, we might not need
to move against each other, not even want
human expressions on our faces,
blank in the green mirror.

If we could cast ourselves again,
echo that first perfect curve
of back, flank, tail, grass-shadow,
we might not need
even water, might feel
the mirror-body grow from our ribs
easily, and not cry out, not needing
to name it lover, child, mother,
sister or stranger.

Tonight I will listen to all the voices,

the deep choir and the ragged solos,
letting them come round me in a circle
where I crouch with my stained cup and my candle.
On my knees I shall lever open
the iron door of the woodstove and gently feed it
rotten logs, hear the wet hiss, see spiders
run from the hot ashes, while outside in darkness
snow will be falling through all the branches.
The lake will be frozen at its edges
into monstrous bearded watchers,
the summer's rushes brittle as the backbones
of starving creatures. I shall sit waiting
in the sweet smoke and the silence, and they will come
shrieking, crooning, clearing their thick white
throats for the intimate whispers.
I shall stretch my cold feet to the embers
and fold my stiff hands and listen
for the creak and groan of ice
as the heavy heads soften and topple.
And if they tell me I am kind
I shall stroke all the fine icicles
at their napes, remembering my own children.
And if they tell me I am ugly
I shall undress for them,
show them my melting body,
address them fluently in their native languages.

The Ark Speaks

As I lay open, you animals
entered me, male and female,
the slavering bull with the ring
came into me, and the cow, the dog,
the sleek bitch; the twin swan-necks
stroked my bare ribs to a gleam
of feathers. Your hooves,
cloven and uncloven, in a cacophony
of echoes; your slow
paws padded across me,
your ingenious beaks
pecked at loose splinters.
In distant passages, what lashing
scales, what scratches,
what lurching victory
of fur, your exotic couplings! You
requisitioned me, crusted my hull
with droppings as I rang
to your screeches. The roaches
swarmed in me, your foul straw mounted
in a steaming bounty
of trapped gases: male and female
lay twitching. And the waters receded
like sleep, my keel nested in branches.
A door creaked, a hand opened. Like an arrow
the raven flew straight out of me.